Copyright © 2018 Tekkan
Artwork Copyright © 2018

All rights reserved.
First Printing, 2018
ISBN 978-1-7324107-4-9

To contact Tekkan please email:
buddhaboy1289@gmail.com

Table of Contents

Dragonfly . . . . Page 3

Lascaux Caves . . . . Page 8

Tour de France . . . . Page 15

Circles of Sober Alcoholics. . . . . Page 74

How to Read My Poems

I have married the sonnet to the tanka. I tell a story in the sonnet — using three quatrains, separated by line spaces, and a final couplet. The story builds to a conclusion in the couplet. The tanka is a commentary, or a counterpoint, to the sonnet — the combined poems have two endings.

I don't rhyme my sonnets, because I want freer expression. I want to be direct in my meaning — I want people to clearly understand my meaning. The metaphors are inspired by Shakespeare, and the (aimed-for) precision is in imitation of Japanese style. Using the sonnet with the tanka, I am mixing the sensibility of the Occident and the Orient — which I have done by living in England, Japan, and America.

I don't punctuate much in my poetry. I want the words themselves to do the work. There is logic between words, and the forms provide structure. By not using punctuation I hope to direct readers to carefully attend to each word — to appreciate the graininess of words.

Reading my poems silently, say, on a bus, a train, or an airplane, and reading them aloud, may be different experiences. The way I've written there's not always a pause intended at the end of the line. Hint: *My poems are to be recited not as lines, but as phrases, and a phrase often overflows the break at the end of a line. I pause and take a breath where it seems natural for me to pause. Another person may pause differently than I do.*

Each single poem is a piece of a mosaic, and it is my hope that the collection of poems form an accurate portrait of consciousness.

My daughter, Jocelyn MacDonald, is a wonderful artist. Her art work graces this book.

I am Barry MacDonald. I received the *dharma* name, *Tekkan*, which means, Iron Man, a settled practitioner of great determination.

— *Tekkan*

Everyday Mind V

A summer morning
fog is obscuring my way —
driving downhill to
meet my friends again in
my familiar Stillwater.

Where ever understanding arises
Ignorance retreats at least for a while
Perhaps because I don't know whether I'll
Remember what I've learned in my next life

Because I know that I'm strung as taut as
Guitar strings pegged at one end needing to
Succeed in business pinned at the other
Persistently feeling lonely pegged by

Middle age and pinned with modest income
And pinned with political views out of
Tune with the establishment and pegged to
A sense of mission and pinned to Buddhist

Compassion and pegged with partisanship
And I'd like to produce some harmony.

I wonder how much
of me I will inherit
with my next body —
will I be curious and
will I be meditating?

Dragon Fly

You are a puzzle piece you are a bug
Born and living underwater for years
You can migrate over the oceans and
With two sets of wings you can angle each

Wing separately allowing you to fly
Sideways and backwards quickly and you can
Hover and you are a predator with
Three hundred sixty degree vision that

Sees colors people can't imagine and
You follow a single bug in a swarm
Snatching and tearing off its wings and with
Serrated mandibles eating in air —

I've wondered why the mosquitoes exist
And it seems they're here for you to gobble.

I can learn about
your abilities I can
marvel over your
exquisite composition
but you can't comprehend me.

Dragonflies have been evolving over
Three hundred million years and their heads are
Wrap-around eyes that see all directions
And each eye has thirty thousand facets

And each facet creates its own image
That combines into vision that gauges
Movement and sees colors beyond human
Capability making them super

Predators that can snatch a fly in flight
That can tear the fly's wings off and hold the
Fly in air with its legs while the dragon-
Fly is hovering with its four wings while
The dragonfly is cutting the fly in bits

By slicing with serrated mandibles —
But I don't believe it has emotions.

Imagine people
with wrap-around eyes instead
of faces — could we
gauge each other's emotions
could we fall in love?

If I could see as a dragonfly does
If I could see a mountain range with the
Rainbow spectrum a dragonfly does I'd
Marvel at the mountains the sun and the

Flowing clouds I'd appreciate beauty
But such colors don't exist for me and
I suppose in the mentality of
A dragonfly beauty has no purpose

And as a fly has no vocal cords it
Doesn't scream as a dragonfly rips off
Its wings so I wonder whether it knows
Horror as people do because people

Are capable of bug ferocity
Sometimes without a smidgen of regret.

Time runs off in both
directions — evolution
designs exquisite
killing machines — and yet I
take heart because of beauty.

The dragonfly has everything it needs
To be a dragonfly meaning it needs
Colors that I can't imagine meaning
There are aspects of reality I

Can't imagine and I don't imagine
A dragonfly needs sentiment as I
Use sentiment so the dragonfly needs
A spectrum of colors while I employ

A spectrum of emotions that makes me
Speculate about a superior
Consciousness with a wider array of
Emotions a deeper intelligence

I can't imagine and I wonder what
Such busy intelligence is doing?

I know just enough
to want to know more to need
to know more but if
it's unimaginable
which direction do I go?

Lascaux Caves

Cave art in France from seventeen thousand
Years ago is pregnant with hints as the
Bison horses and lions together
Are believed to be on the plains and the

Bulls horses deer and bears are supposed to
Be in forest and there is an ibex
A rhinoceros a feline apart
And artists used scaffolding to reach the

Ceilings and they prized yellow red and black
And they swabbed and blotted and sprayed with a
Tube and even as we stand where they stood
Their language is dissipated but were

They moved to create by desire and
Pride by their dreaming or perhaps pleasure?

Fire in the cave
illuminated rock
and generations
collaborated in
recreating life.

Carbon dating the tools pointed to the
Paleolithic era but the age
Of the art can not be determined and
Animals predominate but trees — and

Grass aren't depicted — and we've given names
To the Nave the Apse the Hall of Bulls and
The Chamber of Felines — but we don't know
The words they spoke — but the bulls and bison

Are stamping the horses' hooves are pounding
An archer is thrusting a knee forward
Confronting a line of deer charging and
The life presented bespeaks a throbbing

Heart and surging blood — but their manner of
Greeting and courtesy have disappeared.

Light and breath coming
with tourists introduced
fungus and black mold
so scientists are striving
to contain the corruption.

The camera on the craft Voyager One
Was turned around for a final shot of
The earth four billion miles behind as it
Proceeded to interstellar space and

Once the photo arrived it was filtered
And magnified and in a ray of light
Earth appeared as a pale blue dot prompting
The cosmologist Carl Sagan to

Say every human — ever — lived on a
Mote of dust suspended in a sunbeam
And he considers the poignancy and
The belittlement of human conceit —

Perhaps the miracle of consciousness
Could be explained with more than five senses.

We are spheres of
consciousness extending
only so far and
becoming aware of
vast ignorance.

Nothingness is a thing that's hard to grasp
As I close my eyes and sample blindness
And put fingers in my ears and pretend
To be deaf and a question emerges

Somehow vision became necessary
And the universe created eyesight
Sometime hearing became important and
And ears appeared to drink in sounds and I

Wonder whether the stars and sight arose
Simultaneously and where they came
From — anyway it's easy to marvel
At the flying of a bee humming bird

Putting a beak in a red blossom and
Comprehend exquisite vitality.

Everywhere I turn
I can see iridescence
and hear symphonies
but I also grow weary
and forget about beauty.

Total Solar Eclipse

Even though the differences in size and
The distances involved are understood
And the force of gravity propelling
The moon and earth about each other and

Around the sun is accurately known
And even though we know nowhere else in
The solar system do the orbs align
So much like hand and glove for the moon to

So exactly block the sun in passing
With just a rim of light escaping — the
Miracle is that waves of photons flow
In space into the biology of

The eye and somehow sight and consciousness
Come together and comprehend the facts.

For me seeing the
sunlight passing through
cottonwood leaves and
making me happy
is a miracle.

It's not obvious because the view from
Inside my head and my experience
And my secret thinking convince me of
My individuality and of

My boundaries but from a another point
Of view I can see we are a creature
With billions of eyes with a life spanning
Millennia as we have risen from

Living in caves to Sky Towers as new
Discoveries are passed among us and
I can't predict our direction and my
Comprehension is a pinprick in the

Fabric of space/time but together the
Body of humanity is growing.

The predation
among people
is a disease that
hasn't quite killed us
as we are evolving.

While it's true my history is a trail
Of behavior that puts me here today
And it's true I'm faced with choices only
I can make and it's true my emotions

Resemble the focus of my world but
It's also true my emotions more or
Less aren't much different from my fellows'
And while I seem to be independent

From others I want to remember the
Words I'm using are common currency
And the wellspring of my motivations
Come from the people I admire and

My thoughts are amalgamations of
What other people communicated.

If I were alone
words would be useless
emotions would be
rudimentary
lacking refinement.

Tour de France

As if they were designing a rocket
With the intention of landing on the
Moon a subset of mechanics has been
Busy developing bicycles with

Cutting aerodynamics with feather
Weight with frictionless performance aiming
For continuous improvement over
The previous models because they are

Serving a species of athletes and a
Collection of enthusiasts who love
Bicycle races who love combining
The rigor of competition with the

Magic of evolving technology
Who love the pursuance of perfection.

The bicycle suits
are breathable stretchy and
light as a feather
flamboyantly colorful
wind cheating fashionable.

Some are tall and bulky and their muscles
And hearts are suited for the sprint to the
Finish and some are from high altitude
Nations and they are as slight as birds and

They specialize in ascending mountains
But the rider capable of winning
The three week race must be alert for the
Cross winds that can split groups of riders must

Know when to race and when to follow must
Climb the Alps well and must be able to
Assume the arrow posture of the time
Trial bike and race against the clock alone

Because to win the Tour de France he must
Master the sport with a will to triumph.

He must dedicate
himself to exertion
must leverage the
pinnacle of bodily
strength in turning pedals.

They know every inch of the mountains they
Climb because they scout the sharpest turns the
Grueling gradations and tucked in the back
Of their jerseys they have a radio

And with a headset they talk to the team
Manger about strategy and each
Rider of the team understands his role
In supporting the leader by lining

Up and conserving his energy with
A slipstream so he's ready at the right
Moment to launch himself to attack the
Strongest climbers of the day because the

Point of the team is to protect their best
Rider — his victory is their doing.

The corporations
funding the teams are aiming
to embed the names
of their companies in the
minds of a mass audience.

Teams of riders come with an entourage
Larger than rock bands with a chef a bus
And mechanics and throughout the race the
Riders are followed by team cars with a

Manager co-opting live videos
From the media to appraise himself
And direct his riders by radio
And if someone has a flat tire there are

Support cars with extra tires bikes and
Even shoes — and once Marcel Kittle fell
And needed a new bike while waiting and
Losing time and he busted a shoe too —

He was bruised bloody and impetuous
Changing shoes while pedaling with one leg.

There's no place for a
leading rider to hide on
the Tour de France and
fanatic dedication
precludes humiliation.

The race has become sophisticated
And the teams are lubricated machines
But riders must pedal themselves and the
Mountain slopes of the Pyrenees and Alps

Loom over each rider as there are days
Of ascending three mountains a day and
Each rider must turn the corners of the
Roads and keep pace with the best dancing on

Pedals and everyone tries not to crack
But when descending everyone tests the
End of courage as there's no protection
From harrowing speed from challenging turns

From bone shattering falls apart from the
Perfection of aerodynamic skill.

The bicycles are
fifteen pound machines
and the riders are
flesh and blood athletes
overcoming mountains.

Sprinters are bulky and not suited for
The mountain stages but they must finish
Within a time limit and there are days
Of meandering in sunflowers cornfields

And lavender or along the coast in
The morning in the afternoon when the
Peloton doesn't hurry until it's
Time to organize as teams form in lines

As distance to the finish is measured
And a rapid tempo is established
And sprinters conserve energy within
A slipstream and the leadout men peel off

One by one as positioning happens —
And the winner sprints across in a blur.

Eight hours of racing
two hundred kilometers
come down to fractions
of inches as position
at the end is critical.

Almost every day a group of riders
Breaks away early from the peloton
Stretching a lead to ten minutes and these
Riders from the rival teams need to work

Together each one taking a turn in
Front slicing wind for the others because
Such a small group will soon exhaust itself
As the peloton keeps grinding on and

Almost always the peloton decides
To organize in a line and run down
The rebels and they almost always do
As one by one insurgents crack but some

Days because of timing or terrain or
Cussedness a breakaway hero wins.

Winning a stage of
the glorious affair takes
teamwork even with
rival riders up until
the final fifty meters.

There's a green jersey awarded to the
Rider winning sprints and polka-dot for
Winning mountains and white for the best young
Rider but yellow goes with the fastest

Accumulating time requiring
Leaders to be masters of strategy
Speedy in the solitary racing
Of time trials and dancers up the mountains

Because the one with the yellow jersey
Must be consistently at the front in
Rain and over cobblestones and after
A fall and he must be in the leading

Group split by a crosswind because winning
For three weeks is a difference of seconds.

Racers are handed
bars of nutrition in eight
hours of racing and
everyone sometimes has to
take a pee behind a tree.

Watching the tour on T.V. on the couch
Is the pinnacle of summer splendor
For me as riders sweat up the Alps and
Pelt down gargantuan slopes and pedal

Between fields of sunflowers and follow
Streams in and out of shady trees and grace
Medieval castles and manors along
The way and I don't have to schlep up a

Mountain myself and wait all day to watch
Them pass just once but I can drink coffee
And listen to expert commentary
While sitting on a cushion as they take

The final laps on the Champs-Elysees
After weeks of toil — and sprint to the end.

As the caffeine
circulates in my blood
and my heart beats
a healthy rhythm
I am participating.

I remember the navy blue jerseys
Of the U.S. Postal riders in line
Protecting Lance Armstrong on the mountains
On the plains as he won the Tour de France

For the seventh time and I remember
His teammate Floyd Landis winning a Tour
Too but the glory dissolved when Floyd was
Caught breaking rules by taking drugs and in

Bitterness Floyd revealed that Lance and his
Team were cheats also as they were using
Performance boosting drugs every year of
Every victory as they devised tricks

To evade the tests as cheating was just
Another necessary skill to win.

Once there's cheating
once cheaters win
how can riders
compete without
competing?

I Am Bumble

Some people are asking why I'm calling
Myself Bumble and I say I like the
Buoyant "b"s surrounding the u and m
Because it sounds as if the two "b"s are

Stretching the string of a bass guitar and
When enunciating Bumble the umm
Arises in air reverberating
And warming my tummy and it isn't

So long as to seem grandiloquent but
Its briefness is pithy even puckish
And it's not a name that's commonly heard
So it's unlikely to be forgotten

Easily and I like the idea
Of people saying look here comes Bumble.

Saying names is
a call and response
game and I'm
introducing
variety.

I can do so many things with my phone
Like send email and read the news on the
Internet and listen to music while
Exercising but I especially

Depend on the navigation system
When going somewhere new on the highway
And there are settings within my app where
I can select the shortest or the least

Congested route but I don't fool with the
Settings but there came a day when we were
Late on the way to a wedding and the
Robotic woman's voice sent us to a

Strip mall and told us we'd arrived but we
Were lost adrift and disoriented.

Maybe the snafu was
in the application or
the satellite or
the monotone woman was
just being emotional.

I was on my own with the cilantro
As I didn't know how much of the stems
To keep with the little leaves so I tore
The leaves from the stems with my fingers and

Put them in the bowl — and I cut into
A squishy mango and discovered it
Had a hard core but I finagled the
Knife and put squares of mango in the bowl —

And I was surprised that avocados
Also have a hard core but I chopped up
Four and put them in the bowl along with
A pineapple and green onions and one

Jalapeno pepper without the seeds —
And then I sprinkled on some lemon juice.

Everything was
an experiment
for my début at
David's summer salsa
extravaganza.

I would like to say I'm considerate
And capable of solving world weighty
Controversies but I'm more likely to
Scratch my chin while strategizing how

To get the attention of my friends — but I
Won't be critical because I know it's
Natural to linger smack dab in the
Middle of me — and while preparing for

David's salsa extravaganza I
Discovered mango and pineapple and
Blue berries go well together and adding
Cilantro green onions avocados

And lemon juice is marvelous and while
Stirring it all — my mind became the bowl.

On my own I would
be as likely to chew on
a cottonwood leaf
as a bunch of cilantro —
I don't know what's eatable.

Yesterday to meet a friend of my friend
I drove fifty miles to Menomonie
Wisconsin to Jake's Supper club where I've
Never been and I was rushing on the

Highway because time slips away from me
And I drank more coffee than I should and
Stopped at a rest room with an eye on my
Watch and I was excited not nervous

Because I was exploring because my
Friend created a shimmering image
In my head because I was turning a
Corner with joyful anticipation —

Sometimes reality is a bubble
Bursting and I readjust with a smile.

Adrenalin
possibility
anticipation
are fun before
revelation.

My smooth skin and glossy hair disappeared
A while ago and it can't be said I
Am tall and I wonder how my friend
Described me to his friend and whether when

I emerged a shimmering image of
Romeo popped like a bubble and it's
Unfortunate because once the bubble
Bursts the fun of imagination is

Gone and reality bites but when I
Remember how much I didn't know and
How sloppy my attitudes were when I
Was young and when I see how age turns each

Of us into worn shoes I'm grateful my
Experience allows me to listen.

Words and stories
reveal whether
experience
was enlightening
or a waste of time.

Her mother was cremated in June and
Family and friends assembled for a
Ceremony at the cemetery
And a little box was put in the ground

And before the hole was recovered with
Dirt Marina put a book — the same book
Her mother read to Marina before
Sleeping — next to the box in the hole and

In October while Marina was in
The passenger's seat of an ambulance
While she was doing her best to rescue
Others there was an accident on the

Highway and Marina full of life was
Killed and it just doesn't seem possible.

Marina
eager and
cheerful
is gone.

Saturday morning is like the first day
Of vacation for me because I free
Myself from the demands of absorbing
And manipulating information

Of serving a partisan readership
Who are expecting affirmation and
Insight — but on Saturday morning I
Forget about my mission and cavort

And I don't have to impose opinions
And it's not necessary to be right
And I enjoy my friends whatever they are
Thinking because we gather to pursue

In meditation — quiet extending
In all directions — in-between thinking.

The quiet flows
continuously
and it's seldom
as demanding as
the past or future.

It's never been so crowded as I stood
Half in and out of the door waiting in
Line at the coffee shop on Saturday
Morning after mediation but I

Didn't mind because our Zen contingent
However slowly was advancing and
Mixing with others we didn't know and
I enjoy watching people — anyway

After a session of practiced quiet
Gabbing comes naturally and today
Paul captivated conversation by
Telling a story about scouting in

A town of secretive polygamists —
Who could predict such a turn of events?

Pouring caffeine on
top of meditation is
a wonderful way
to finish off a Saturday
morning — who knows what's coming?

I was given a pair of castoff clogs
In the spring and they're a smidgen big for
Me but I love the ease of slipping them
On and I don't have to bend over and

I only have to stick my feet in and they
Are so like a pair of slippers with an
Inch and a half soles that give me that much
More stature and once summer arrived I

Stopped wearing socks and I'm celebrating
The season by also wearing the most
Colorful silk shirts while typing these words
In my short pants with my knees bent and with

My feet arched and my naked heels up
Luxuriating in the summer air.

Once in a while a
little stone will find its
way under my foot
so I raise my toes and it
falls from my clog easily.

Each of us has a special conception
Of entertainment and nutrition and
Of what's appropriate for us and I'm
Grateful because he's helping out around

The house as he spots movement and follows
With his eyes as his ears go forward as
He tenses and springs and scrambles and swipes
And lunges and paws as well as he can

And I'd say he's as limber and precise
As a ballerina but he's frantic
In pursuit with not a hint of grace or
Discipline and he's pleasure to watch —

None of the others could do what he did
As Kit Cat caught and ate the nuisance fly.

Which was better
catching or eating
the fly — I
couldn't do it not
without seasoning.

Kit Cat is a miniature mountain lion
And after eating he ignites and jumps
On the refrigerator and gallops
In the house and wrestles with Johnnie as

Johnnie flops on his back and keeps Kit at
Bay with his legs — and everyday Kit Cat
Assumes the role of supremo but I
Was puzzled to see Kit's ears were scabby

And I couldn't guess how he came by his
Wounds until I saw Johnnie on his back
Kicking with his hinds legs at Kit's face as
Kits was reaching for a part of Johnnie

To bite but Johnnie wiggled and twisted
And nailed until Kit Cat strutted away.

Kit is a cat of
commotion and nerve
and Johnnie is
watchful quiet and
full of surprises.

Hi — I'm bloviation alcoholic
So don't pay much attention to me as
I get a kick listening to myself
As you suspect a lack of substance in

My words but communication is how
I keep from drinking so please indulge a
Little gas as I think the future is
Not what we suppose but does resemble

A tiger jumping from behind and we
Don't know what's coming and often we
Are not prepared and the past doesn't trail
Behind us but is everywhere before

Us and we just can't stop remembering
And what we remember isn't healthy.

A sober drunk
may be sensitive
and self-conscious
and with sobriety
may become vainglorious.

Cancer is a tiger pouncing on an
Unsuspecting soul from behind and it
Doesn't happen to everyone all at
Once but one by one and the division

Between observing and getting sick is
Like being on a body of water
On the periphery of a whirlpool
And proximity is an illusion

As over time everyone encounters
The deadly circular current leading
To the abyss as far as we know but
Mixing with the preponderance of fear

Is the potential for growing a heart
Emanating the gift of compassion.

We can't seem to do
without enduring fear but
buried within is
also a capacity
for growing compassion.

I've grown accustomed to bearing the load
Of living with people as I'm paying
The mortgage the car and the telephone
Bills and car insurance is sensible

But health insurance is a government
Racket so I'm doing without it and
I'm familiar with the summer lull and
Autumn resurgence of cash coming in

Peculiar to my business and this year
I'm working around a tax penalty
Due to a late payment and I'm learning
How to put my financial concerns in

A box in my mind as I'm doing my
Daily routine helping me feel normal.

So many people
need to be paid and
most of them I don't
know but I'm the same —
I need to be paid.

The dog days of summer never came this
Year as the air was clear and mild and now
It's already chilly at sunrise and
Twilight — near the ending of August — and

This morning I see the foliage of trees
In Stillwater is barely stirring and
There's not a single bird under a sky
Heavy with grayish clouds gradually

Disappearing — but I don't care because
By this afternoon I'll be driving in
Town with the windows open and I'll be
Walking in my short pants feeling the warmth

Of the sun on my bare legs — I don't have
The time to think about cold days coming.

There are hints of
bare trees and
lacerating wind
I'd rather not
think about.

Plato's Cave

I was dreaming and facing the rock wall
Of a cave chained and unable to turn
To see the fire behind me and all
I could see were the shadows of people

Dancing on the illuminated stone
Before me and I felt the weight of my
Slavery and an urge of my body
Compelled me to rise from bed and stumble

To the bathroom to pee while I was half
Dreaming and half awake marveling in
A twilight trance imprisoned but wanting
To escape my ignorance to break the

Chains and emerge from the depth into the
Sunlight — where I could feel the wind flowing.

Plato believed the
visible world is only
an illusion and
what he called the ideals
exist beyond our grasping.

Mom found it in an envelope box while
Dusting bookshelves and I saw spots of age
On the cover as she hesitated —
Because I can be cranky — but this was

Dad's doctoral dissertation that he
Came to American to write as he
Wanted an education and in these
Pages remain his youthful pursuit of

A rational basis for faith and we
Knew the millennia of scholarship
The culmination of effort these typed
Words are as he tried so hard to be a

Messenger of wisdom and a leader
For people who were trying to be good.

Mom is a faithful
guardian of each issue
of fifty years of
publishing a journal that
Dad and I did together.

I remember pondering in autumn
The meaning of melancholy when I
Was young during my drinking days when I
Liked the twilight season in between the

Sunshine the rippling water and the
Wildflowers and the inescapable
Cold — because a drinker savors sadness —
And a turning from the light to gloom is

Familiar — but with the layering on
Of thirty years I've learned to savor the
Party colors of the leaves differently
As marks of time and reminders of

People and places disappearing like the
Leaves dissipating in a bracing wind.

I'm not savoring
notions of sadness
I'm remembering
what really was but
isn't any more.

I have to keep coming back — otherwise
I could resort to a bicycle or
A donkey — because this is what we do
To fill our tanks with gasoline because

I'm expected in St. Paul in forty
Minutes and calculating the distance
The stoplights the traffic the construction
On the highway I've got no time to waste

So here I am at Neighbor's Stop again
And soon I'll have to take my mittens off
Because they're too bulky and insert my
Credit card with freezing fingers and

Once the nozzle of the pump is in the
Car I watch the numbers of the price rocket.

The combustion of
gasoline speeds me over
distances as corn
fields and strip malls arise and
disappear before my eyes.

I see an apple tree in front of a
Modest home with crooked and trimmed branches
That's on my route to Bayport — and I've seen
It in February decorated with

Christmas bulbs providing a bleak season
With a little cheer — and in April in
Passing I've seen the apple blossoms
Reminding me of beauty — and in the

Summer it's easy to forget because
It's just a little tree among the more
Imposing trees — but this autumn I do
Remember it because I remember

Apples come from apple trees and nothing
Is better in autumn than ripe apples.

The Christmas bulbs
hung in the apple tree are
ornamental fruit —
but the apples in autumn
are natural fruition.

On the verge of September the sun is
Still a resplendent presence in the sky
And on the edge of sixty years of life
My body is phenomenal but the

Symptoms of asthma that I carry were
Triggered this year by the drifting smoke of
The wildfires in California and in
Oregon and my breath is constricting

And I'm lucky to have medicine and
I'm determined to work around tightness
Of breath when necessary and I don't
Think about my horizons very much

But at the pinnacle of my health I
Am reminded everything is passing.

Asphyxiation
wouldn't be much fun
but whatever
happens I'm looking for
continuing horizons.

I try to bring my thoughts down to a low
Simmer and if successful I'm aware
Of sights and sounds and so I've noticed while
Walking my left ankle pops sometimes and

So does my left index finger and if
I were in a funk I'd never hear how
Peculiar my bones can be but when I
Try to make my joints crack it doesn't work

So it's not possible to create a
Rhythmic jingle and I'm not even sure
Whether bone or cartilage snaps or
If humidity or temperature

Is responsible but I will listen
Carefully for the next permutation.

I suppose
big old Paul
has a bass knee
I have a tenor ankle.

The everyday world is coy while I go
About my business thinking about a
Dozen things I don't want to see blossom
Into problems but I escape pressure

By taking time in the morning to play
With words while I have clarity because
I so often do cross a threshold of
Satisfaction that carries me through the

Day but to keep playing I depend on
A split second of recognition when
I see something funny or worthy of
Remembering as a starting point so

Within the happenstance of everyday
I am a hunter of hidden marvels.

Inspiration came
in the church sanctuary
as we were quiet
walking and meditating
I heard my ankle snap.

At a gathering of my family
My mom reminded me of Louie our
Miniature black poodle we named after
A French King and I haven't thought of him

For fifty years and only my mom and
I knew Louie who had a high-pitched bark
Who wouldn't be quiet sometimes and we
Remembered how he sprang through the front door

When he could and my brother my sister
And I chased him as he ran in frantic
Circles pleased that he was free until he
Tired and it's funny how words can spark a

Memory and I'm back on a tree-lined
Boulevard within Hutchinson Kansas.

There's a place in my
head where Louie was waiting
to be remembered
and he's running in circles
again until I get tired.

Indian Summer

If I were to epitomize a day
Of my life saying this is what it feels
Like to be alive I suppose I could
Come close to an ideal by dwelling in

A September afternoon because as
I remember the air is often mild
And the sky is sunny and the clouds drift
Lazily and I'm comfortable in

A t-shirt and I could pick an apple
Off a tree and eat it and even as
The mornings and evenings are becoming
Chilly and the night is lengthening the

Warmth of a September afternoon makes
Me believe everything is provided.

The year always comes
around to a September
afternoon again
but I recognize comfort
is temporary.

Sometimes a diagnosis comes without
Possibility of recovery
With palliative care the only option
And I can't imagine how I would feel

If told of multiple lesions large and
Deep within my brain that brought the loss of
Coordination and concentration
As I'm sure I'd have premonitions but

The words coming from a doctor would be
A pronouncement of the end coming more
Quickly than expected but leaving time
Enough for preparations and choices —

With time enough to remember the good —
To compose myself — and to say goodbyes.

I think I've been
preparing for the
eventuality
of my transition
but I'm not ready.

I resolve to identify something
Worthy of remembering everyday
Whether it be a memory — like how
I heard a British student use the word

Worthy when I was in England and I
Realize I'm been imitating him
Ever since — or whether it be a way
Of seeing — like what would I do if I

Were given a dead end prognosis with
Little time left — because I believe so
Much of life slips by while I'm consumed
With trivialities — that I resolve

To calm my mind and to open my eyes
And identify something that's worthy.

Everyday
opportunity
rises with the sun —
something will be fresh
and I'll play with words.

The word tamongoes isn't accurate
As people call them tomatoes and what
Good is a word if people don't know it's
Meaning and I don't know why it came from

My mouth and maybe something is amiss
In my head but I like the sound of ta-
Mon- goes because it has an exotic
Flavor that makes me think of mangoes that

Have a hard core while the tomatoes are
Runny but both are sweet and juicy and
Both fit within my hand — anyway when
Some of us gathered around the table —

To look at what Lee brought to give away —
I liked the shock of saying tamongoes.

It's fun to defy
Expectations by
Behaving strangely —
When you say poodle
I'll say elephant.

Once caffeine enters the calculation
A peak and valley must be expected
And I do find myself attached to my
Morning cup of coffee — believing what's

The point of a sunrise without a boost
Of stimulation — and after sips and
A little time I am limber and am
Ready at my desk summoning the words —

Half of me becomes a receptive eye
Absorbing as much of my presence as
Possible and half of me becomes a
Response that rises from somewhere and if

I am especially nimble the words
Settle into place without confusion.

The force of my
concentration
opens a window —
opportunity
quickly dissipates.

Would it be beneficial to know what
People are thinking in the privacy
Of their heads while their expressions may show
Contentment or agreement would it help

Me to know with certainty whether they
Are bored and preoccupied with something
Not my business because it's enough for
Me to manage the promptings of my own

Thinking as I know my face and words do
Express a false front sometimes as I try
To be in harmony and the question
Whether it's necessary to be frank

Or better to be courteous is a
Choice that's an everyday predicament.

My impassive eyes
are watching carefully for
the subtlest clues
in your changing expressions —
just as you're watching me.

I feel the strain of keeping pace with the
World and meeting the expectations that
Come with my job and with the people in
My life as I depend on money and

Friendliness to go on and sometimes I
Get agitated thinking I'm cornered
By what people want from me and by what
I want that isn't happening and I'd

Like a different life but don't know what to
Do as I'm looking for direction and
Patience but even on a cloudy day
I notice the morning is beautiful

As I'm taking time and absorbing the
Covering of the mother-of-pearl clouds.

Sometimes I'd like to
jump out of myself
but where to go is
the conundrum so
I'll keep being me.

My Japanese Zen master expressed a
Quiet dignity not dependant on
What people thought of him because he was
Purposeful and he pointed to the need

In daily practice to forget the self
By mixing with the moment completely
And he would say if fearful be fearful
If irritated be irritated

And he didn't mean to be unkind to
People but he said it's important to
Experience the emotion clearly
To face difficulty without running

Because there is no separation from
What is and I would realize the truth.

Preoccupation
with self-criticism or
self-condemnation
is putting another head
on top of my working head.

And my Japanese Zen master said we
Americans need to learn to chew the
Words of masters more than we do because
Chewing aids the digestion and the words

"Study the self to forget the self to
Drop body and mind and be enlightened
By the myriad things" are said to be
Legitimate and worth considering

And he also said study the moment
And I've made a practice of attending
To whatever comes to mind as it comes
Without evasion because he said the

Forgetting of the self happens in an
Instant and can only happen right now.

Practice depends
on poise and
receptivity
even if emotion
has me in a grip.

A fog enveloped the trees and homes of
Stillwater before the sun rose and I
Saw only the shadows of things because
Of the street lights I passed while driving and

I loved the solitude and wanted to
Put my energy to use and it seemed
The fog represents the true face of the
World that over a familiar landscape

I've grown exhausted with if I depart
From my habitual activity
Uncertainty is pervasive and if
I keep my eyes open and attend to

What emerges new possibilities
Could present themselves if I am ready.

I believe the world
is pregnant with
possibility
but I've become
habituated.

I remember picking apples from a
Tree in the neighborhood when I was a
Kid and the skins were crisp and the fruit was
Fresh and juicy and all my life apples

Have never tasted as good as those when
I was roaming Bayport in a t-shirt
On a bicycle without a care — but
As I'm driving through Stillwater watching

The leaves blooming with color — I think of
Red and yellow apples and realize
It takes winter spring summer and fall to
Bring apples to fruition — and for me

Autumn becomes a juicy ripe apple —
A culmination of the shining sun.

As my rootedness
in years has brought me
understanding of
natural fruition
and its evanescence.

Photons are invisible scientists
Say and the brain exists in darkness yet
Somehow energy is flowing in the
Eyes the nerve cells the synapses and the

Visual cortex and somehow sunlight
And starlight reveal the vastness of the
Universe and the speed of light and space
Time has been calculated but there is

No explanation for how I have a mind
That sees and comprehends the miracle
Of my mother's motherly concern for
Her gladioli and geraniums

And chrysanthemums that expresses a
Nurturance underlying everything.

Consciousness expands
until it bumps against its
limitations and
devolves to geraniums
and chrysanthemums.

I blinked with realization after
I forgot to file my business taxes
So I raced to my accountant and we
Filed quickly and then I received a

Notice from the I.R.S. demanding
A thousand dollars and my accountant
Said taxes weren't owed and he'd write a
Letter and the penalty wouldn't stick

But I received another letter and
I considered why my signature was
Necessary just to prove I'd read it
And then I discovered two weeks warning —

They will break my door and seize property
Unless I pay a thousand dollars fast.

Sometimes I find
visions come to mind
and I'm seeing
I.R.S. agents
falling from airplanes.

I saw some teenage boys haggling on
The street as they were organizing a
Game with a ball and bat that led me to
Remember how boys will argue and shout

How aggression determines dominance
And the pack apportions the status of
Each and I remember my brother and
I roamed the neighborhood on bicycles

And we joined the other boys in games of
Football and baseball in empty lots and
We knew the rules because we watched the pros
Who were gods in stadiums on T.V. —

And I remember Harmon Killebrew
Swinging his bat for another home run.

I remember
Tony Oliva
running and stretching
for a long fly ball —
perfectly graceful.

I would like to thank my friend for showing
Me how easily my ego bruises
On Saturday morning — even after
Meditation — when we gathered at the

Coffee shop at our usual table
As I thought we were having a lively
Discussion and I was insightful and
He was looking at me and listening

But then he responded to someone else
Revealing he was looking at me but
Attending to others and it took a
Little time to laugh at myself because

I do exactly the same thing and need
To practice lessening my importance.

It's a burden to
be needy of attention
when people are
already accepting me
and what more do I want?

Sometimes the moon is big and other times
Small and it may look orange or silver
Depending on circumstances and on
My own I wouldn't understand but I

Know its orbit is elliptical so it
Comes closer to and farther from the earth
And I know on average it's about
Twenty thousand miles away because I

Discovered the facts on the Internet
And I've learned the moon's gravity keeps the
Earth from wobbling and thereby we have
Reliable seasons and I think it's

Marvelous we live with a burning sun
An orbiting moon and ripe tomatoes.

The sun is ninety-
three million miles
away and I am
happy it is not
nearer or further.

The Bench Press

It was a thing I happened upon that
Set me apart from others that gave me
Encouragement that I could lay on my
Back and lower a heavy barbell and

Successfully lift it when most other
Teenagers couldn't that got me into
Wrestling that got me used to life long
Exercise that gave me a goal in my

Thirties to press three hundred pounds while I
Weighed one hundred and forty that I worked
Hard to accomplish and one day I got
The bar half-way up a little higher

On the left side which was always stronger
And I came close but finally couldn't.

I trained as hard as
possible and took my shot
and afterwards I
knew my opportunity
was vanishing with time.

There is a constant ringing in my ears
That I notice when I choose to notice
And for years I meditated while in
The bedroom next to mine Joshua was

Playing video games with who knows whom
On the web and making electronic
Racket but I got good at not hearing
Nuisance noise — though I did have to shut him

Up whenever he was swearing — but then
Once I settle within my posture an
Energy arises and everyday
I discover the magic of focus —

Consciousness perpetuates energy
And there's no telling where I am going.

A black zafuton
and a black zafu
filled with buckwheat
are my connection
to the universe.

I sit on the edge of turbulence and
Serenity and find that silence is
Theoretical as there is always
A dog barking and traffic humming in

The distance just as nothingness is an
Idea hard to wrap my arms around
And while I'm teetering on the edge my
Attention has to go somewhere and it's

Impossible to banish sensations
And I can't often predict when a thought
Will give rise to a line of thinking that
Will be difficult to dislodge without

Effort but whatever comes to mind I
Practice watching the moment being.

A lot can happen
in forty minutes
even though I am
not moving — my mind
is hovering.

I was attracted to a type of the
Silk shirts at the thrift store and bought about
A dozen and a friend pronounced the name
Of the style but I didn't catch the word

And was too embarrassed to admit my
Ignorance within the circle of my
Friends but I understood that the style was
Cuban so I called them my garbanzo

Shirts for a joke to prompt my friend to say
Guayabera again and that's how I
Got the name and that's how I discovered
A joker can get away with a lot —

But I must admit I really didn't
know the meaning of garbanzo either.

I thought garbanzo
was an appellation for
a mafia goon
and I was being clever
until I looked up the word.

I'm not pretending to be the smartest
Or the wisest but I enjoy playing
With words because I find satisfaction
In constructing little lines of words and

In stacking them upon each other to
Make walls of words that serve as pictures of
Moments in a life and it's possible
To clarify what experience means

And today I find autumn has many
Voluptuous connotations as the
The occasion of ripe tomatoes and
Apples and suddenly the leaves are

Are on fire with color on the days of
Indian summer before winter comes.

It's fun to be
spontaneous
as I grasp at
geese fixing them in
v formations.

Autumn is dissolving again as leaves
Are scattered on the ground crumpled and brown
And this morning I see leaves collecting
With the rain spattering in the puddles

Along the street and I am watching the
Sweeping of the wipers clearing the rain
From my windshield allowing me to see
Autumn dissolving again as I go

To meet friends again as I do every
Morning regardless of the season as
My routine is my stability and
I often go to the same place at the

Same time to see familiar faces and
Laugh as autumn is dissolving again.

I drink coffee and
am perky in the
morning in every
season as my blood
is circulating.

Who could blame Mr. Bean for snoozing in
His folding chair while he was alone in
An empty museum in uniform
As a security guard puffing with

His lips fluttering and then his back slipped
Down the metal chair and he almost slid
Out of the chair while his mouth was open
And then he bent forward with his chest just

About touching his knees and he wavered
On the edge of the chair on the verge of
Collapse but he found a precarious
Point of balance and then he snorted and

Startled and rose back into the chair with
His arms dangling and he was still asleep.

Mr. Bean was
a human noodle
who gave himself to
child-like foolishness
to make people laugh.

Equinox

This is not the end as there is no end
But the harvest moon this October is
A symbol for me of the frictionless
Motion of the orb that functions as a

Mirror for the sun that is a marker
For the equal division of day and
Night on a predictable schedule as
A balancing of sunlight and starlight

I appreciate — and I see crumpled
Leaves on the grass with the light of an
Orange moon as round as a pumpkin
As it rises in twilight and becomes quite

Stunning transforming into a silver
Luminous moon traveling in the night

Chinese poets
centuries ago
left traces of
themselves with words of
moonshine Zen and wine.

Circles of Sober Alcoholics

Come with a story and take your turn as
One of us welcome within the circle
Meeting every morning for an hour and
When we're done we'll disperse to our lives with

A renewed sense of purpose because it's
Not about beating the obsession with
Alcohol for most of us but about
Living differently finding confidence

Discovering the inspiration to
Be useful and productive and once in
A while I'm pleasantly surprised because
I realize how much I've changed from the

Miserable drunk with a splitting head
To an optimist exploring today.

It's our purpose with
stories to encourage those
obsessed with drinking
to show it's possible to
overcome the urge to drink.

I know a guy on a spiritual path
Meaning he's trying to be sober and
On the night of a lunar eclipse he
Resolved to take the time to watch as a

Shadow passed across the moon because he
He thought seeing the event would make him
Happy and he persevered until the
Moon appeared again full and luminous

But he was disappointed because he
Invested his time and effort because
He couldn't see himself as we see him
Grasping for the moon and being silly

As emotions come and go and it takes
Time to learn that emotions come and go.

The moon is
in the heart and
a passing shadow
takes its time but
the moon is in the heart.

Ordinary or trivial is how
He imagines the lives of most people
Believing perhaps there's not much to be
Discovered or inspired by as he's

A lawyer and routinely meets people
At their unhappiest and as he's just
A little cynical and talks about
Changing his profession I think he's snared —

I wish him greater dissatisfaction
He's not unhappy enough to pursue
The wholehearted search for inspiration
As loneliness cuts away illusions

As urgency sharpens perception as
Intuition arises he'd transform.

Sleeplessness helped me
pay attention to my thoughts
restlessness pushed me
to seek something meaningful
providing satisfaction.

Did you learn to swallow emotion as
You drank and did your drinking assume a
Mysterious compulsiveness crossing
Boundaries and making limitations

Of time or quantity laughable and
Did the drinking come to a horrible
End and a tenuous ambivalent
Sobriety — And have you discovered

A mysterious division between
Everyday events and your emotions
As if you were a troubled child learning
About anger for the first time — to be

Sober it's necessary to face the
Emotions you evaded through the years.

Sobriety is
the barest beginning of
a new way of life —
once anger is surrendered
forgiving is natural.

It's not the first time he's been acknowledged
For staying sober for a length of time
And it's our custom to give medallions
Signifying the months or years and to

Hear from him about how sobriety
Was achieved — and so he tells a story —
And as we go around the circle and
Everyone has a say we cheer him with

Stories and you may not comprehend our
Happiness — he has a bowl of six-month
Medallions and thinks he should return them
Perhaps being confused about failure

And success as he sees only the months
While we appreciate the many years.

We remind ourselves
we have a mission to do
not to drink today
and if there is only shame
there's no room for saving grace.

We haven't seen her for months and it's so
Predictable that she would say as she
Did say that she intends to come again
Regularly and we know that as she's

Saying the words she really means it and
Yes it is possible in a moment
To make a resolution and to be
Sober going forward but we also

Know that saying the words is not enough —
It takes an unbearable amount of
Pain to stay quit before the obsession
To drink and some of us never seem to

Cross the mysterious threshold within
And surrender to God and become safe.

To be one of us
to be one who doesn't drink —
it's not about pride
it's about surrendering
and opening completely.

It's a curious blindness that he can't
Appreciate the gift he gave us in
Speaking truthfully about the abuse
He suffered at the hands of his family

That he would reveal the hole in his soul
That no subsequent accomplishment could
Fill as he also told of successes
Worthy of the world's shallow envy but

The hunched over posture of his body
His absence from a later gathering
And the pain obvious in his words point
To the continuing oppression of

Suffering as it's most difficult to
Overcome neglect during a childhood.

But that's why we come —
to achieve transcendence of
the suffering and
together to turn it to
penetrating compassion.

It's a new world if you're attempting to
Stay sober that appears the same on the
Surface but you'll notice the emotions
Are more painful as if you're a turtle

Who's lost his shell and your skin is tender
And there are people who are angry and
Hurt because of your actions and there's the
Necessity of admitting your wrongs

And repairing the damage and taking
The time to understand the world through the
Eyes of others and so perhaps you'll find
Yourself in a hall of mirrors seeing

Distorted images of whom you thought
You were and discovering you don't know.

It's exploration
attempting to stay sober
and engaging with
life's difficulties — maybe
you'll discover who you are.

It was surprising to realize how
Habitually resentful I had
Become as I was disconnected from
Everything as my mind transformed into

A funnel focusing repeatedly
On why I should be upset excluding
Every mitigating factor and I
Was impervious oblivious and

Cherished justifications and my thoughts
Circulated malignant obsessions
As fuel for alcoholism as I
Drank to escape poisoned thinking — only

Compassionate sober alcoholics
Could transmit the way of sobriety.

The companionship
and shared experience of
my fellow addicts
helped me to surrender my
useless justifications.

Even within the circles of sober
Alcoholics as I gazed about the
Group during those first tenuous months
And years I would catch myself daydreaming

How much happier I'd be if I were
Clever like her or tall like him but I
Knew they're addicts just like me and I had
Greedy eyes and I was compulsively

Comparing myself with them even as
They came to the circles for survival
And I don't know how it happened because
It's a mysterious process but I

Mixed myself with sober alcoholics
And discovered how lovable I am.

The stories and words
had cumulative effect
as I stopped caring
about what I didn't have
and found a home among friends.

During those first few years it felt as though
I were walking out of my life into
The rooms where there was a circle of the
Most welcoming people and addiction

And alcoholism were left outside
With the associated compulsions
And run-away emotions and the so
Dangerous events that had to be faced

While inside we told each other stories
That only fellow-addicts could savor
Properly and we shared a way of life
That fosters transcending growth involving

The replacement of failing habits with
Intuition and appreciation.

As the years have passed
I've come to think differently
And feel differently
And my outlook is open
And my days are engaging.

More than most drunks he has reason for self-
Pity as a young son died suddenly
As grief and anger are persuasive and
So much has disintegrated where's the

Blame in spiraling out of control and
Where's the leverage for trusting a God who
Took a son and yet he's returned to a
Room full of sober alcoholics he's

Listening as we share about hitting
Bottom about how each of us crossed a
Threshold of suffering and surrendered
How together we seek sustenance from

Power beyond ourselves — guidance from a
Wisdom salvaged in the midst of despair.

There's no comparing
of personal suffering —
was it sufficient
for me to surrender and
did it force me to seek help?

He said he went to the casino on
Sunday evenings because the rookies had
Been playing the slots all afternoon so
He went to clean up and in the midst of

His compulsivity while drinking he
Remembered becoming disgusted with
A machine and leaving for another
And colliding with another gambler

On the way and what bothered him today
Was that he said nothing and walked on as
If the other person was nobody
And so many years later within a

Circle of sober alcoholics he
Regretted a moment of rudeness.

Even in the midst
of compulsivity and
a haze of drinking
an addict recognizes
there's a better way to live.

Her husband took many photos she said
And for ten years since his death she's felt a
Reluctance in looking at them because
She wasn't proud of the things that happened —

There was the photo celebrating her
Last day of work at the hospital and
Though she was laughing and cavorting she
Knew how out-of-control drunk she was then —

Here was the denial the stubbornness
The misery she perpetuated —
But there were also the photos of her
Grandchildren who never knew her drinking

During ten years of sobriety — she
Discovered evidence of redemption.

She knew the inside
story of every photo
the pretense and the
reality but she
forgot being redeemed.

I'm a lucky alcoholic who's found
A home within my head and heart and I
Don't have to drink to escape myself and
Don't have to hide from my emotions and

I've learned the tricks necessary to take
Disturbing circumstances and adapt
And I'd rather have a conversation than
A confrontation and I'm more likely

To be spontaneously happy than
Sullen for no explainable reason
Because I've been practicing spiritual
Jujitsu by paying attention to

The quality of my thoughts and often
It's easy to adjust my attitude.

In conversations
with sober alcoholics
I discover ways
of minimizing ego
and letting go of trouble.

I come to mix within the circle of
Sober alcoholics every morning
And the meeting is where my friends are — it's
Where we laugh — and sometimes someone will

Say they have a relative who doesn't
Understand why we come to meetings when
We haven't been drinking for years and it's
Not easy for normal people to see

If I lose my gratitude I'd also
Lose my sobriety and — it's a fact —
Someone in the room is certain to be
Desperate not to drink today and it's good

To bear witness to the suffering and
To communicate how to get sober.

I'm idiosyncratic
and have outlandish stories
that only sober
alcoholics could enjoy
because we've gotten sober.

There are consequences for giving up
If you are alcoholic and you leave
The circle of sober alcoholics
Who have learned to rely on the meetings

Because within any group some of us
Are suffering and others are serene
And as we share experience strength and
Hope the needed words are said and we leave

Encouraged — and as I was exiting
The highway in St. Paul I saw a man
Panhandling on the street and he saw
Me and turned as the recognition was

Painful for both of us — but it's a fact
Those who quit coming become examples.

A bad attitude
stubbornly defiantly
indulged is enough
to send an alcoholic
on the road to his demise.

In circles of sober alcoholics
We laugh spontaneously as we swap
Stories as we enjoy ourselves and make
Light work of sobriety because we

Aren't isolated aren't suffering from
The poisoned thinking characteristic
Of drunk fools so when she confided how
Her father took her to a hospital

How she heard him talking to a nurse in
Another room saying "I don't want her
Anymore" how he tried to leave without
Her but failed we sober alcoholics

Became quiet because we could see the
Budding alcoholism in the girl.

There are stories we
would rather not remember
but we can't forget
so we muster up courage
and tell each other the truth.

Her parents left her behind at a gas
Station and at a swimming pool and they
Didn't intend to hurt her but worse they
Forgot she was one of the family —

And though they retrieved her they also gave
Her the impression she's worthless
And now the grown woman can't get enough
Attention to lose the expectation

She is forgettable — just as if she
Were given a piece of a puzzle and
Assigned the burden of finding where it
Belongs — so it seems she's been abandoned

She's lost and upset and struggling to
Compose herself and to find the way home.

To compose herself
to discover the way home
is quite a puzzle —
in a world full of strangers
to find those who are loving.

We're not all capable of understanding
Each other as I've heard him say that the
Newspaper the television and the
Radio impart private messages

And his skin is continuously stamped
With the imprint of God — and the Devil
Is a presence tormenting his thoughts — and
Jesus is a Savior today and though

We breathe the same air we don't receive the
Same stimulus and he's articulate
Enough to use words rational enough
To describe his thoughts passionate enough

To specify a reality so
Unrecognizable I can't respond.

Perplexity and
passionate intensity
have come together —
he understands just enough
to perceive his separateness.

We finished on Friday afternoon when
Usually our crew would return to
The yard at twilight and I was happy
To be done with asphalt driveways and I

Showered and ate and went to the bar alone
At the beginning of a holiday
Weekend on the Fourth of July — I was
Elated to be young and strong but was

Lonely too amidst strangers feeling out
Of place so I drank like a fool shots
Of tequila and I remember a
Glimpse of lying in a police cruiser —

Of being showered at Ramsey County
Detox — and of waking with a split head.

The drinking was an
attempt at overcoming
disconnection — but
at the time my behavior
was quite unexplainable.

I became an exciting driver near
The end because I never knew where I'd
End up or who I'd meet in the night and
One evening I found myself blundering

In a field though I'd been aiming at the
Road and I sped up — I have a hazy
Recollection of meandering home —
And the last night I sped up a hill in

Stillwater took a sharp turn and faced a
Lighted police cruiser while my friend in
Exasperation was grasping my neck
Politely obliging me to stop so

I went to jail which displeased me so I
Asked to be taken to detox again.

For alcoholics
once drinking's begun there's no
control of how much
of how long or of what could
eventuate on the way.

So much of my experience depends
On my outlook and I found myself at
A detox center again discussing
The situation of my arrival

With earnest volunteers who suggested
Bad things happen when alcoholics drink —
But there is a solution — and I felt
The resistance within vanish — and the

Shame was lifted from my shoulders and for
More than thirty years I've not had a drink
Because in an instant I surrendered
And became willing to do anything

For a better life — and for decades I've
Watched people die before surrendering.

Why was I able
to surrender while many
others couldn't — what's
the mysterious edge
favoring my life?

We discussed how sober alcoholics
Are likely clueless about knowing when
Enough is enough because we often
Want more whether it be excitement or

Praise for our deeds or quantities of goods —
Because why buy one when you can have three? —
And Larry said we are the best worst guys
Or the worst best guys — anyway if we're

Passionate we're compulsive too and don't
Recognize the compulsion and can't be
Otherwise unless somehow we learn to
Jump outside ourselves and see exactly

What we're doing so it helps to bounce our
Separate perspectives off each other.

Because we remain
addicted to excitement
and want to be the
center of attention and
avoid mundaneity.

He told us about being lost in the
Gobi but he wasn't disconcerted
Because he had a guide who knew how to
Bark like a dog and listen — and the guide

Drove over the dunes and stopped and barked and
Listened and drove again — as the stars were
Spectacular — and eventually
They heard the barking in the distance of

A sheep dog leading to the ger of a
Family where he could do what he came
For — to provide medical care — and then
They were directed to Ulaan Baater

Ingenuity will find direction
Wayfarers use sheepdogs in the desert.

A clear head
a willing heart
patience and fortitude
allow unlimited
adventure.

Deer Hunting on Sunday

It's quite cold before dawn — he said — and the
Hollow was much colder and he heard drops
Falling from the trees but couldn't see much
In the gloom — but he remembered how good

The warmth of the sun feels when the body
Is chilled — so with the sun rising with the
Light filtering through the trees he rose and
Walked up hill looking for an opening

And up ahead he saw a log within a
Showering of light and the moisture in
The log was escaping and steaming and
Just for a moment an iridescence

Arose hovering and shimmering and —
The once-in-a-lifetime vision vanished.

He shared his vision
and he shared his gratitude
that he was sober
that he could appreciate
clarity and redemption.

More than a few of us in the circle
Dread the approach of Christmas because the
Season reminds us of regrettable
Memories and sometimes our parents and

Siblings are out-of-control drinkers and
We'd rather not be gathered together —
But he reminisced about the cookies
His mother baked for Christmas of a Czech

Recipe consisting of flour and ground
Walnut — but this year she was ill and in
Bed and he volunteered and he followed
Instructions and when he and a sister

Opened a paper bag of the cookies
They smelled the years of sweetest memories.

Some alcoholics
lug the baggage of Christmas
but sharing stories
is a way to rekindle
buried enthusiasm.

Such things too
the smudges
on slabs

take part in
the bloom —

row apartments
and vine roses.

(Remembering our one-time home in Japan.)

— *Tekkan*

www.ingramcontent.com/pod-product-compliance
Lightning Source LLC
Chambersburg PA
CBHW052104070526
44584CB00017B/2325